# THE ROLE OF
# Pastors & Christians
## IN CIVIL GOVERNMENT

## DAVID BARTON

Aledo, Texas
www.wallbuilders.com

*The Role of Pastors & Christians in Civil Government*
Copyright © 2003, David Barton
1st edition, 3rd printing, 2007

**Additional materials available from:**
WallBuilders
P. O. Box 397
Aledo, TX 76008
817-441-6044
**www.wallbuilders.com**

**Cover Painting:**
Doug Latta
Tulsa, OK

**Cover Design:**
Jeremiah Pent
Lincoln-Jackson
235 Wenner Way
Ft. Washington, PA 19034

Library of Congress Cataloging-in-Publication Data
323.4
Barton, David
The Role of Pastors & Christians in Civil Government.
Aledo, TX: WallBuilder Press
56 p.; 21 cm.
Endnotes included.
A transcript of the video and audio by the same title.
**ISBN 10:** 1-932225-03-X
**ISBN 13:** 978-1-932225-03-7
PN6122
1. American Speeches   2. Patriotism   3. Freedom of Speech   4. Democracy

Printed in the United States of America

# The Role of Pastors & Christians in Civil Government

A quote attributed to President Woodrow Wilson forcefully pronounces:

> A nation which does not remember what it was yesterday, does not know what it is today, nor what it is trying to do. We are trying to do a futile thing if we do not know where we have come from, or what we have been about. [1]

WOODROW WILSON

This is true with America today. We have forgotten where we have come from and what we have been about, and this is especially true when it comes to the role of the church – of ministers and Christians – in the civil arena. Strident voices both inside and outside the

Christian community assert that Christians never have been involved in the civil arena and should not be now. Many Christians have even embraced this constricting mentality by adopting a compartmentalized view that allows them to express faith and values in church but then divorces those same faith and values from the civil arena. The teachings of the Bible reject this compartmentalized approach to life, and our history demonstrates that for generations Christians embraced a different viewpoint.

An excellent indication of how much Americans have forgotten their own history occurs around the Fourth of July. If you ask most citizens why America separated from Great Britain, the overwhelming response will be "taxation without representation." That answer is acceptable – as far as it goes, but taxation without representation was only one of twenty-seven grievances listed in the Declaration of Independence; and it was actually one of the lesser of the twenty-seven complaints.

Listed in the Declaration eleven times more often than taxation without representation was the abuse of representative powers; the abuse of military powers was listed seven times as often; the abuse of judicial powers four times as often; and stirring up domestic insurrection twice as often. Taxation without representation was merely grievance number seventeen out of the twenty-seven, listed alongside Great Britain's suppression of immigration and her interference with our foreign trade. The taxation issue was given little emphasis in the Declaration, yet it is the one issue that everyone knows about today. Why aren't most Americans familiar with the rest?

The reason is that in the 1920s, 30s, and 40s, a new group of historical penmen began writing in America. They included Charles and Mary Beard, W. E. Woodward, Fairfax Downey, and many others. Apparently believing that the only motivating factor in life was money, they began to teach American history with that emphasis, introducing what is now called the "economic approach to American history," authoring

books such as *The Economic Basis of Politics*. [2] They also presented the economic basis of the Constitution, the economic basis of the Revolution, and, in other words, economics became _the_ basis. Since the sole economic clause in the Declaration was "taxation without representation," this became the one clause that Americans have learned about in their history books for the past half-century.

Today, after two generations of having been taught that economics is the only thing that matters, behavior now seems to conform to that viewpoint. For example, forty-five percent of the evangelical Christians who voted in recent elections said that economic issues were more important than moral issues. And our national leaders too often today are judged not on the basis of their personal competency, moral character, or other leadership traits but rather on the basis of how the economy is doing, what the unemployment rate is, or how the Dow Jones Industrial Average is performing. Yet, a reading of American history textbooks prior to these recent writers – in fact, just a reading of the twenty-seven reasons given in the Declaration – will present a completely different view of history from that which is taught today. It will reveal that other more important issues motivated most individuals.

For example, in 1762 America's very first missionary society was chartered: "The Society to Propagate the Gospel among Indians and Others in North America." [3] Americans thought this was a great idea but King George III apparently thought that it would compete with the work of the nationally established Church, so he vetoed the charter. [4] This type of action by the King alarmed a number of the Founders who contended for religious liberties in America – including the ability to start their own missionary societies, Bible

BRIEF ACCOUNT
OF THE
Society for propagating the Gofpel
among the *Indians* and others
IN
NORTH-AMERICA.

CHARTER OF AMERICA'S
FIRST MISSIONARY SOCIETY

societies, or Sunday School societies. Consequently, Founding Fathers such as Charles Carroll of Carrollton and Samuel Adams, both of whom became signers of the Declaration, cited religious freedom as a reason they became involved in the American Revolution. [5]

There was also the issue of slavery. In 1773, Pennsylvania passed a law to help bring slavery to an end, [6] and other Colonies were also making attempts to end slavery, [7] but King George III vetoed those American laws. [8] The King was pro-slavery; the British Empire practiced slavery; and as long as America was part of the British Empire, it too would practice slavery. This position by the King was a source of great discontent for many Founders. Henry Laurens, a President of Congress during the American Revolution, protested against this British position:

I abhor slavery. [But] I was born in a country where slavery had been established by British kings and parliaments . . . ages before my existence. [9]

HENRY LAURENS

Since the only way for America to end slavery was to separate from Great Britain, many Founders believed that separation would be an appropriate course of action. In fact, in the drafting of the Declaration of Independence, Thomas Jefferson personally penned the clause declaring:

THOMAS JEFFERSON

[King George III] has waged cruel war against human nature itself, violating its most sacred rights of life and liberty in the persons of a distant people who never offended him, captivating and carrying them into slavery in another hemisphere or to incur miserable death in their transportation thither.... Determined to keep open a market where men should be bought and sold, he has prostituted his negative for suppressing every legislative attempt to prohibit or to restrain this execrable commerce. [10]

KING GEORGE III

That is, not only has King George III engaged in slavery and the slave trade but he has even opposed all efforts to stop it. Ending slavery was so important to so many of the Founders that when America did separate from Great Britain in 1776, several States began abolishing slavery, including Pennsylvania, [11] Massachusetts, [12] Connecticut, [13] Rhode Island, [14] Vermont, [15] New Hampshire, [16] and New York. [17]

It is true that not every State immediately abolished slavery; and it is also true that even though the overwhelming majority of Founding Fathers were anti-slavery, not all were. In fact, Jefferson's forceful denunciation of the slave trade in the original draft of the Declaration was complained about so strenuously by the delegates from Georgia and South Carolina that his clause was removed from the Declaration [18] and a milder condemnation inserted instead. Nevertheless, the desire to end slavery was a major factor in the thinking of many Founding Fathers.

For example, America's first anti-slavery society was founded in 1774 with the help of Benjamin Franklin and Dr. Benjamin Rush [19] (both of whom became signers of the Declaration of Independence). This society was founded two years before the separation from Great Britain – an act of civil disobedience, for King George III had said America could not end slavery.

THE
CONSTITUTION
OF THE
Pennsylvania Society,
FOR PROMOTING THE
ABOLITION OF SLAVERY,
AND THE RELIEF OF
FREE NEGROES,
UNLAWFULLY HELD IN
BONDAGE.
BEGUN IN THE YEAR 1774, AND ENLARGED

But these two Founders ignored that dictum and worked to end slavery anyway; and Dr. Benjamin Rush led the anti-slavery fight for almost four decades [20] and even headed the national abolition movement. [21]

For many Founders, their desire to end slavery was religiously motivated. This fact is illustrated by John Quincy Adams, who hated slavery and so crusaded against it that he was nicknamed "the hell-hound of abolition" [22] for his unrelenting efforts to abolish that evil. In a famous speech, [23] Adams cited the Bible passage from Luke 4 where Jesus declared that he had come to "proclaim liberty to the captives";

JOHN QUINCY ADAMS

he then noted that if this was the goal of the Savior, it should also be the goal of all Christians – they, too, should work to end slavery. [24]

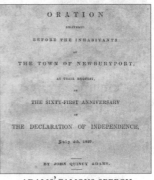

ORATION
DELIVERED
BEFORE THE INHABITANTS
OF
THE TOWN OF NEWBURYPORT,
AT THEIR REQUEST,
ON
THE SIXTY-FIRST ANNIVERSARY
OF
THE DECLARATION OF INDEPENDENCE,
July 4th, 1837.
BY JOHN QUINCY ADAMS.

ADAMS' FAMOUS SPEECH

Clearly, issues such as religious liberties and the desire to end slavery – as well as the removal of trial by jury, the impressment of American seamen by the British, the placing of the military power above the civilian power, and many others – were important reasons behind the Founders' separation from Great Britain. Yet all that most Americans hear about today is "taxation without representation."

Another indication of how little is known today about our own history is revealed when Americans are asked, "Who were the leaders most responsible for the movement in America that led to our independence?" Today, we hear names such as Samuel Adams, the "Father of the American Revolution"; [25] Thomas Jefferson, the principal author of the Declaration; John Hancock, the President of Congress with his bold signature on the Declaration; and John Adams, who not only signed the Declaration but who also negotiated and signed the Peace Treaty with Great Britain to secure our independence. These were indeed important political leaders behind our independence, but previous generations also knew about other important leaders.

ADAMS' SIGNATURE ON THE 1783 PEACE TREATY

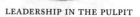

John Adams himself declared that the Rev. Dr. Jonathan Mayhew and the Rev. Dr. Samuel Cooper were two of the individuals "most conspicuous, the most ardent, and influential" in the "awakening and revival of American principles and feelings" that led to our independence. [26] Other ministers whose influence and leadership were also important included the

JOHN ADAMS

Rev. George Whitefield, the Rev. James Caldwell, the Rev. John Peter Gabriel Muhlenberg with his brother the Rev. Frederick Augustus Muhlenberg, and many more. [27] (The exploits of many of these ministers are recorded in several older historical works, including *The Pulpit of the American Revolution*, [28] *The Patriot Preachers of the American Revolution*, [29]

LEADERSHIP IN THE PULPIT

and *The Chaplains and Clergy of the Revolution*. [30]) Regrettably, today we don't hear much about the role of the church – of ministers and Christians – in the founding of our civil government.

Why could John Adams say that pastors in particular (and Christians in general) were so influential in our move for independence? It was because of the work of pastors in shaping the thinking (i.e., the worldview) of the nation, and because of the work of Christians in founding our government. Consider first the impact of pastors on America's thinking (worldview) two centuries ago.

Today, Christians agree that the Bible relates to every area of life, but in the Founding Era this relevance was demonstrated in a manner unfamiliar to most Americans today. This is evidenced by examining the published sermon topics of earlier generations. A published sermon represents only a small fraction of all the sermons preached in those days. Today, sermons are taped, filed, and reproduced on demand; two centuries ago, it cost a considerable amount in both time and money to publish even a single sermon, so unless the demand for a sermon had been especially high from those who heard it, it was not published. Therefore, a published sermon was probably a sermon that had a significant, life-changing impact on the listeners.

The topics of early published sermons demonstrate that the church truly believed – and taught the nation – that there was nothing in life that the Bible did not address, directly or indirectly. For example, in 1755, when New England suffered an earthquake, the sermons following that event addressed – earthquakes! In other words, the Church said, there has just been an earthquake; what does the Bible teach about such an event? The Bible says so much about this subject that this was actually a five-part sermon about earthquakes. [31]

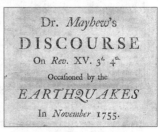

A sermon five years later was on the Great Fire in Boston. [32] That is, there's just been a tragic local event; what principles does the Bible provide to deal with this tragedy? (Both of these sermons were preached by the Rev. Dr.

Jonathan Mayhew, one of the ministers specifically cited by John Adams as influencing our independence.)

Another sermon concerned an eclipse. [33] Most Christians probably have never heard a sermon about a solar eclipse; yet that sermon is filled with verses specifically addressing eclipses. The Church taught the nation a practical Christianity – no matter what oc-

curred in any area of life, consult the Bible, it had the answers.

Although this sermon is from 1851, and obviously not from the Founding Era, it still maintained a relevance to life. Notice the topic:

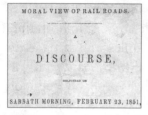

"A Moral View of Railroads." [34] This minister pointed out that railroads were a part of transportation, and after he discussed what the Bible taught about transportation, he then showed how railroads fit into God's overall transportation plan.

Returning back to the Founding Era, another sermon topic was "The Infirmities and Comforts of Old Age." [35] While all know that aging has its challenges, this is not a popular sermon topic today. But since aging has been going on from the beginning of mankind, doesn't it seem likely that God might offer advice on the issues of aging? Indeed He does – and it is pointed out in this sermon.

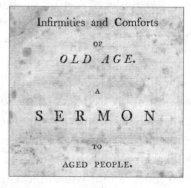

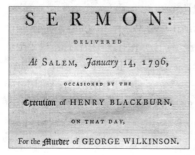

Many sermon topics from two centuries ago might cause consternation today. One such sermon was an Execution Sermon. [36] This particular sermon was preached on the execution of Henry Blackburn for the murder of George Wilkinson. Often such sermons were based on

CIVIL JUSTICE

Romans 13 in which the Scriptures declare that God has given the sword to civil government. These sermons would investigate whether an execution was a proper use of the sword by civil government. All of the above sermons were considered "occasional sermons" – that is, they were sermons preached because of a significant occasion. Another class of sermons was called "annual sermons" – sermons on a specific topic, preached annually.

One annual sermon was called an Artillery Sermon. [37] Once a year the local military assembled together and had a minister address them to lay out from the Scriptures the proper role of the military. This

ADDRESSING THE MILITARY

clearly is a Biblical subject, addressed in both the Old and the New Testaments; even John the Baptist had specific instructions for soldiers and officers as he was baptizing.

Another type of annual sermon was called an Election Sermon, [38] the longest traditional form of annual sermon in America. The first documented election sermon was preached in 1634 in Virginia, [39] and for each year thereafter until the twentieth century, election sermons were preached in pulpits across America. Christians understood their dual citizenship. They were indeed citizens of heaven, but they were also citizens of earth. God had placed them here in America with a stewardship government that belonged to "We the People," so what did God expect from them in their stewardship capacity concerning the civil government that He had given them? What did He expect from them in the selection of their leaders? What did the Scriptures teach about the election process? For almost three centuries, this was a topic addressed annually in pulpits across America.

S E R M O N
PREACHED BEFORE
His Excellency JOHN HANCOCK, Esq.
GOVERNOUR;
His Honor SAMUEL ADAMS, Esq.
LIEUTENANT-GOVERNOUR;
The Honourable the
COUNCIL, SENATE, and HOUSE of
REPRESENTATIVES,

Many of these annual sermons directly involved the Founding Fathers. For example, such sermons were regularly preached before John Hancock (signer of the Declaration and the first Governor of Massachusetts) and before Samuel Adams (also a signer of the Declaration and the first Lieutenant Governor of Massachusetts) and before the

SIGNERS OF THE DECLARATION

Council, Senate, and House of Representatives of that State.[40] (Many States began their legislative session by inviting a minister to preach a sermon addressing the Biblical principles regarding lawmaking. The Bible truly offers much guidance on this topic, for not only is

PRAYER IN CONGRESS

God the Great Lawgiver but many heroes of our faith were also lawgivers, including Moses, Joseph, and Daniel.)

Many sermons preached in legislative chambers were attended by a number of our Founding Fathers. For example, one was preached before Samuel Huntington,[41] the Governor of Connecticut and a signer of the Declaration of Independence. Another was preached before Caleb Strong,[42] the Governor of Massachusetts and one of the delegates at the Constitutional Convention and a framer of the Constitution. Another was preached before Oliver Wolcott, [43] the Governor of Connecticut and a signer of the Declaration of Independence. And there were many others.

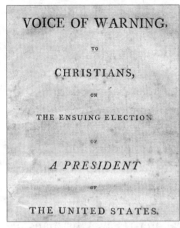

VOICE OF WARNING,

TO

CHRISTIANS,

ON

THE ENSUING ELECTION

OF

A PRESIDENT

OF

THE UNITED STATES.

Another sermon topic was "A Voice of Warning to Christians on the Ensuing Election of a President of the United States." [44] In earlier generations, American ministers stood in the pulpit and called candidates and parties by name, set forth their positions, compared them to the Bible, and then advised that a Christian should or should not vote for a candidate or party based on what the candidate said compared with what the Bible said. Today, this type of sermon might make many listeners in churches uncomfortable, but it shouldn't; not only was this a traditional practice of American pulpits, it was also a traditional practice set forth in the Scriptures.

Consider how often God sent His ministers either to interface with or to confront civil leaders: Elijah with Ahab and Jezebel, Samuel with Saul, Nathan and Gad with David, Isaiah with Manasseh, Jeremiah with Josiah, and so many others. There certainly is no Biblical model where God has His ministers remain silent with civil leaders, or about civil issues.

PROPHETS AND KINGS

The church speaking into the civil arena was a long-standing practice in America, as was the practice of ministers serving directly in the legislature. In fact, it was Thomas Jefferson himself who encouraged the lifting of restrictions against ministers and clergy that had been imposed in his own state of Virginia:

I observe . . . [in the Virginia] Constitution an abridgment
of [a] right . . . I do not approve. It is the incapacitation of a
clergyman from being elected. [45]

Thomas Jefferson wished to see clergymen possess the same rights
as others. Today, however, this is not the case in the area of free speech,
nor has it been since 1954, when a U. S. Senator became responsible for

enacting a policy that treated non-profit
organizations, including churches, differently. [46] He had been criticized for his political affiliations and his private business
dealings and, not liking that criticism, he
added a rider to an appropriation bill in the
U. S. Senate stipulating for the first time
that a 501(c)(3) organization – and churches
are 501(c)(3) organizations – must stay out
of the political arena. Few Christians re-
alize that the current restrictions on free
speech in the pulpit are of recent origin,
but both American law books and early
American sermons clearly demonstrate
that such is the case.

The historical record is clear: the Church helped shape the way that
early America approached the issues of the
day. The nation learned the relevancy of
God's word to every aspect of life; it is not
surprising, then, that the Scriptures – and
expositors of the Scriptures – had such a
profound impact on the founding of our
government and on its documents.

Consider the Declaration of Independence. No nation has ever been
as long under the same founding document as America has under the
Declaration. In fact, France had their Revolution more than a decade
after America did, and she is now in her fifteenth government. [47] Brazil has had seven constitutions since 1822; [48] Poland has had seven

since 1921; [49] Afghanistan has had five since 1923; [50] Russia has had four just since 1918; [51] and the story is similar for other nations. This type of instability has characterized nations in Europe, Africa, South America, and the rest of the world – except America. So where did our Founders find the ideas that made the Declaration the most successful government document in the history of the world? They themselves answer that question.

James Otis – the mentor of both Samuel Adams and John Hancock – declared that:

JOHN LOCKE

The authority of Mr. Locke has . . . been preferred to all others. [52]

Declaration signers such as John Adams, Benjamin Franklin, Thomas Jefferson, Benjamin Rush, and many others also sang the praises of John Locke; [53] and John Quincy Adams declared that:

The Declaration of Independence [was] . . . founded upon one and the same theory of government . . . expounded in the writings of Locke. [54]

Clearly, John Locke had a powerful political influence on America and the Declaration of Independence. Interestingly, critics today classify Locke as a deist or a forerunner of deism, [55] but this is completely erroneous. Not only was John Locke considered a theologian by previous generations, [56] but he even wrote a verse-by-verse commentary on Paul's Epistles and also compiled a topical Bible, which he called a *Common Place-Book to the Holy Bible*, that listed the verses in the Bible, subject by subject. When anti-religious enlightenment thinkers attacked Christianity, Locke defended it in his book, *The Reasonable-*

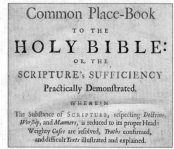

LOCKE'S PLACEBOOK TO THE BIBLE

*ness of Christianity as Delivered in the Scriptures*. And then when he was attacked for defending Christianity in that first work, he responded with the work, *A Vindication of the Reasonableness of Christianity*. Still being attacked two years later, Locke wrote, *A Second Vindication of the Reasonableness of Christianity*. [57] No wonder he was considered a theologian by his peers and by subsequent generations!

However, the writing of John Locke that most influenced the Founders' philosophy in the Declaration of Independence was his *Two Treatises of Government*. In fact, signer of the Declaration Richard Henry Lee declared that the Declaration itself was "copied from Locke's *Treatise on Government*." [58]

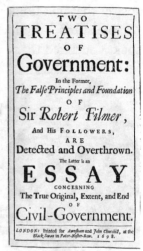

LOCKE'S TWO TREATISES

Even though that book is less than 400 pages long, Locke refers to the Bible over 1,500 times to show the proper operation of civil government! This is the primary work influencing the Declaration of Independence; no wonder the Declaration has been such a successful document!

Our Constitution has also been successful – so successful, in fact, that America is the longest on-going constitutional republic in the history of the world. Significantly, our Constitution was an original and uniquely American document; it was not a compilation of the best clauses of other constitutions from across the world. It contained simple ideas that had never before been embodied in written constitutions – politically new and novel practices such as the separation of powers, checks and balances, and full republicanism. Where did the Founders get their specific ideas for this most successful of all constitutions?

In an attempt to answer this question, political scientists embarked on an ambitious ten-year project to analyze some 15,000 writings from the Founding Era. [59] Those writings were examined with the goal of isolating and identifying the specific political sources quoted during the time surrounding the establishment of American government. If the sources of the quotes could be identified, then the origin of the Founders' political ideas could be determined.

From the 15,000 writings selected, the researchers isolated some 3,154 quotations and then documented the original sources of those quotations. The research revealed that the single most cited authority in the writings of the Founding Era was the Bible: thirty-four percent of the documented quotes were taken from the Bible – a percentage almost four times higher than the second most quoted source. [60]

In fact, signers of the Constitution George Washington and Alexander Hamilton acknowledge that the principle undergirding the separation of powers was the same principle found in Jeremiah 17:9 [61] – a principle that had been the subject of numerous sermons during the Founding Era. Many other Bible verses and principles also found embodiment in the Constitution. For

SIGNING THE CONSTITUTION

example, compare the Art. I, Sec. 8 provision on uniform immigration laws with Leviticus 19:34; compare the Art. II, Sec. 1 provision that a president must be a natural born citizen with Deuteronomy 17:15; the Art. III, Sec. 3 provision regarding witnesses and capital punishment with Deuteronomy 17:6; and the Art. III, Sec. 3 provision against attainder with Ezekiel 18:20. And notice that Isaiah 33:22 defines the three branches of government, and Ezra 7:24 establishes the type of tax exemptions that the Founders gave to our churches (that still exist today). The concept of republicanism set forth in Art. IV, Sec. 4 – that is, of electing our leaders at the local, county, state, and federal levels – has its origins in Exodus 18:21. In fact, Noah Webster, the Founder personally responsible for Art. I, Sec. 8, ¶8 of the Constitution, specifically cites Exodus 18:21; [62] and John Jay and George Washington also attributed God's  providence as the reason that America elected its own leaders. [63]

Since so many of the ideas that found application in our government were taken from the Bible, it is not surprising that John Adams had identified Christians and ministers as being so influential in American independence. Nearly four decades after the American Revolution, he reaffirmed this position, declaring:

> The general principles on which the fathers achieved independence were. . . . the general principles of Christianity. . . . Now I will avow that I then believed, and now believe, that those general principles of Christianity are as eternal and immutable as the existence and attributes of God. [64]

JOHN ADAMS

Significantly, not just John Adams, but many other Founding Fathers and early American political leaders also declared that America was guided by or founded on Christian principles. Among those making such declarations were Elias Boudinot, [65] a President of Congress during the Revolution; and signers of the Declaration Charles Carroll, [66] John Hancock, [67] Benjamin Rush, [68] Stephen Hopkins, [69] and Samuel Adams. [70] Also citing Christian principles as foundational are Constitution signers George Washington, [71] Alexander Hamilton, [72] Rufus King, [73] John Dickinson, [74] and Roger Sherman. [75] Others making similar declarations about Christian principles in America include Samuel Chase, [76] a signer of the Declaration and a U. S. Supreme Court Justice; original Supreme Court Chief Justice John Jay; [77] Justice Joseph Story; [78] Justice James Kent; [79] Zephaniah Swift, [80] author of America's first legal text; [81] and the U. S. Supreme Court itself, [82] not to mention the U. S. Congress [83] as well as numerous

State Supreme Courts and State legislatures. [84] Other famous Americans who claimed that America was a Christian nation or was built on Christian principles included leaders such as General William Eaton, [85] leader of America's first conflict following the American Revolution, and Daniel Webster, [86] the great "Defender of the Constitution." U. S. Presidents declaring that America was a Christian nation or that it was founded on Christian principles included John Quincy Adams, [87] Abraham Lincoln, [88] Woodrow Wilson, [89] Zachary Taylor, [90] Harry Truman, [91] Andrew Jackson, [92] William McKinley, [93] Herbert Hoover, [94] Teddy Roosevelt, [95] and many others. Educational leaders who taught students in classic American textbooks

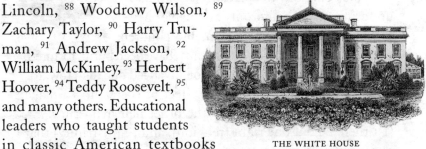

THE WHITE HOUSE

that Christianity was the basis of our country and its government included notables such as Noah Webster, [96] "The Schoolmaster to America," Jedediah Morse, [97] "The Father of American Geography," and William McGuffey [98] of the famous *McGuffey Readers*. All of these, and so many more Founding Fathers, leaders, educators, and official departments of government declared that America was a Christian nation or that it was influenced by or built on Christian principles by Christian leaders.

THE U. S. CAPITOL

It was because of this strong Christian faith that the Founders were willing to welcome those of other faiths to America. The Founders knew the truth of Christianity; they believed that it would prevail on its own merits without the need for force or coercion. As Thomas Jefferson explained:

> Truth can stand by itself.... [W]hy subject [religious opinion] to coercion? To produce uniformity.... Is uniformity attainable? Millions of innocent men, women, and children, THOMAS JEFFERSON since the introduction of Christianity, have been burnt, tortured, fined, imprisoned; yet we have not advanced one inch towards uniformity. What has been the effect of coercion? To make one half the world fools, and the other half hypocrites.... [I]f there be but one right [religion], and [Christianity] that one, we should wish to see the nine hundred and ninety-nine wandering sects gathered into the fold of truth. But against such a majority we cannot effect this by force. Reason and persuasion are the only practicable instruments. To make way for these, free inquiry must be indulged; and how can we wish others to indulge it while we refuse it ourselves. [99]

Consequently, our Founding Fathers openly acknowledged and welcomed the presence of numerous religious groups in America, including Buddhists, Muslims, and Jews. In fact, John Randolph of Roanoke, an early member of Congress from Virginia who served with the Founding Fathers, said that he was personally "in favor of Mohamedanism." [100]

DR. BENJAMIN RUSH

(He was later converted to Christianity and discipled by Francis Scott Key, [101] author of the "Star Spangled Banner." Randolph then became a strong personal advocate for Christianity. [102])

Dr. Benjamin Rush, a signer of the Declaration who served in three presidential administrations, and one of the most evangelical Christians among the Founding Fathers, openly declared:

Such is my veneration for every religion that reveals the attributes of the Deity, or a future state of rewards and punishments, that I had rather see the opinions of Confucius or Mohamed inculcated upon our youth than see them grow up wholly devoid of a system of religious principles. But the religion I mean to recommend in this place is that of the New Testament. [103]

And while describing a federal parade in Philadelphia, Dr. Rush commented:

The rabbi of the Jews locked in the arms of two ministers of the Gospel was a most delightful sight. There could not have been a more happy emblem. [104]

 And Elias Boudinot, a President of Congress during the American Revolution, served as president of the "Society for Ameliorating the State of the Jews," and made personal provision for bringing persecuted Jews to America. [105]

This tolerance for other faiths and religions, however, did not negate nor alter the fact that America was founded by Christians, on Christian principles. In fact, in 1854, following an extensive one-year investigation, the U. S. Congress succinctly declared:

INSIDE THE U. S. HOUSE

Had the people, during the Revolution, had a suspicion of any attempt to war against Christianity, that Revolution would have been strangled in its cradle. At the time of the adoption of the Constitution and the amendments, the universal sentiment was that Christianity should be encouraged, but not any one [denomination]. . . . In this age there can be no substitute for Christianity. . . . That was the religion of the founders of the republic, and they expected it to remain the religion of their descendents. [106]

INSIDE THE SUPREME COURT

Half-a-century later in 1892, the U. S. Supreme Court also conducted a thorough review of American history. After citing more than sixty historical precedents, the Court concluded:

There is no dissonance in these declarations. There is a universal language pervading them all, having one meaning; they affirm and reaffirm that this is a religious nation. . . . this is a Christian nation. [107]

But today's pseudo-historians, not willing to let truth or historical fact stand in the way of their personal secularist convictions, proclaim just the opposite, asserting that neither our nation nor its leaders were influenced by Christianity.

**The Founding Fathers Were *Not* Christians**

Steven Morris

The Christian right is trying to rewrite the history of the United States as part of its campaign to force its religion on others. According to this Orwellian revision, the Founding Fathers of this country were pious Christians who wanted the United States to be a Christian nation, with laws that favored Christians and Christianity.

Not true! The early presidents and patriots were generally Deists or Uni-

of hell) was invited to become an army chaplain, the other chaplains petitioned Washington for his dismissal. Instead, Washington gave him the appointment. On his deathbed, Washington uttered no

"The early presidents and patriots were generally Deists or Unitarians, believing in some form of impersonal Providence but re-

One article declares, "Our Founding Presidents Were Not Christians." [108] Another similarly announces "The Founding Fathers Were *Not* Christians" [109] (notice the emphasis on the word "not"). Another proclaims that the "Signers of the Declaration were Enemies of Christ." [110] The *L. A. Times* heralds "America's Unchristian Beginnings," with an inset box declaring, "The founding fathers: Most, despite the preachings of our pious right, were deists who rejected the divinity of Jesus." [111]

## Los Angeles Times

THURSDAY, AUGUST 3, 1995, METRO, PART B, PAGE 9
COPYRIGHT 1995, THE TIMES MIRROR COMPANY

**America's Unchristian Beginnings**

■ **Founding Fathers:** Most, despite preachings of our pious right, were deists who rejected the divinity of Jesus.

By STEVEN MORRIS

The Christian right is trying to rewrite the history of the United States as part of its campaign to force its view

Universalist who denied the existence of hell, was invited to become an Army chaplain, other chaplains petitioned Washington to reject him. Instead, Washington gave him the appointment.

On his deathbed, Washington uttered no words of a religious nature and did not call for a clergyman to be in attendance.

* John Adams, second President. Drawn to the study of law but facing pressure from his father to become a clergyman, he wrote that he found among lawyers "a noble air and gallant achievements" but among the clergy, the "pretended sanctity of some absolute dunces." Late in life he wrote: "Twenty

flowed from the lips of Jesus himself are within the comprehension of a child; but thousands of volumes have not yet explained the Platonism engrafted on them; and for this obvious reason that nonsense can never be explained."

* James Madison, fourth President and father of the Constitution: "Religious bondage shackles and debilitates the mind and unfits it for every noble enterprise," he wrote. "During almost 15 centuries has the legal establishment of Christianity been on trial. What have been its fruits? More or less in all places, pride and indolence in the Clergy, ignorance and servility in the laity; in both, superstition, bigotry and persecution."

According to these and many other writers, our Founding Fathers were a collective group of atheists, agnostics, and deists; they didn't believe in Jesus; they weren't Christians. And since our Founders were allegedly nothing more than atheists, agnostics, and deists, the title of a current university textbook seems to make complete sense: *The Godless Constitution.* [112]

Many Americans today would not disagree with these characterizations. After all, in the painting of the signers of the Declaration, who are the two Founders that most Americans can immediately recognize? Thomas Jefferson and Benjamin Franklin, of course!

THE SIGNERS OF THE DECLARATION OF INDEPENDENCE

But can they identify which one in the picture is Samuel Huntington – or Robert Livingston, George Clinton, Robert Morris, Stephen Hopkins, Richard Henry Lee, George Read, Roger Sherman, Elbridge Gerry, or the others? Americans seem to know nothing about these other signers.

We have been trained to recognize the two "least religious" Founders, Franklin and Jefferson. While we don't know the others, we nevertheless are told that they were just like Franklin and Jefferson. However, in defense of Franklin and Jefferson, while they may have been the two "least religious" Founders, "least" is a comparative term; even they would be much more religious than most "religious" individuals today.

After all, Benjamin Franklin not only drafted a statewide prayer proclamation for his own State of Pennsylvania [113] but he also recommended Christianity in the State's public schools [114] and worked to raise church attendance in the State. [115] He also desired to start a colony in Ohio with the Rev. George Whitefield to "facilitate the introduction of pure religion

BENJAMIN FRANKLIN

among the heathen" in order to show the Indians "a better sample of Christians than they commonly see in our Indian traders." He enthused, "In such an enterprise I could spend the remainder of life with pleasure, and I firmly believe God would bless us with success." [116] Franklin also made one of the nation's most forceful defenses of religion [117] when it was attacked by Thomas Paine, the author of the infamous *Age of Reason*. And it was Franklin – citing numerous Bible verses to prove his point – who called for the establishment of chaplains and daily prayer at the Constitutional Convention. [118] These are the documented actions of one of the "least religious" Founding Fathers.

And then there is Thomas Jefferson. Not only did he recommend that the Great Seal of the United States depict a Bible story and include the word "God" in the national motto [119] but President Jefferson also negotiated a federal treaty with the Kaskaskia Indians in which he included direct federal funding to pay for Christian ministers to work with the Indians and for the building of a church in which the Indians could worship [120] – and this

THOMAS JEFFERSON

treaty was ratified by the U. S. Senate! Furthermore, Jefferson closed

JEFFERSON – "IN THE YEAR OF OUR LORD CHRIST"

presidential documents with the appellation "In the year of our Lord Christ," thus invoking Jesus Christ into official government documents. [121] And this is Thomas Jefferson – the other "least religious" Founder! Most Americans really don't know that much even about the Founders they think they know best!

But what of the other signers about whom most Americans know less? Of the fifty-six signers of the Declaration, over half were educated in schools established for the purpose of training ministers for the Gospel, and they received what today would be considered degrees from seminaries or Bible schools. [122] Many of the Founders also served as ministers or were active in Christian service.

For example, the Rev. Dr. John Witherspoon was an ordained minister of the Gospel, published several books of Gospel sermons, [123] and played major roles in two American editions of the Bible, including one from 1791, [124]

WITHERSPOON'S SERMONS

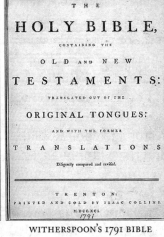

WITHERSPOON'S 1791 BIBLE

considered to be America's first family Bible.

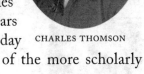

THOMSON'S BIBLE

Charles Thomson was also responsible for an American edition of the Bible still available today. [125] Called *Thomson's Bible*, it is the first translation of the Greek Septuagint into English. It took Charles Thomson some twenty years to complete that work; today it is still considered one of the more scholarly American translations.

CHARLES THOMSON

When Dr. Benjamin Rush died in 1813, he was considered one of America's three most notable Founders, ranking in prominence along with George Washington and Benjamin Franklin. [126] In 1791, this signer of the Declaration founded The First Day Society which grew into today's Sunday Schools. [127] He also helped start America's first Bible society: The Bible Society of Philadelphia. The original constitution for that society was authored by Dr. Rush. [128] In looking for

FIRST BIBLE SOCIETY

ways to print Bibles faster and more economically, Dr. Rush and the Society came across what was called stereotyped printing – an early form of mass production. The result was America's first stereotyped, or mass-produced Bible [129] – and it came about through the efforts of Dr. Benjamin Rush, signer of the Declaration.

Francis Hopkinson was a church music director and choir leader, and the editor of a 1767 hymnal [130] – one of the first purely American hymnals. His work took the one hundred and fifty Psalms and set them all to music so that we could sing the Psalms much as King David had done thousands of years be-

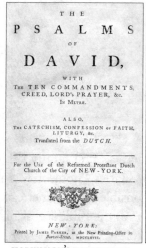

HOPKINSON'S HYMN BOOK

A PSALM SET TO MUSIC

fore – and this unique Bible hymnbook was the work of a signer of the Declaration.

THOMAS MCKEAN

Thomas McKean was one of America's leading legal authorities, responsible for a 1792 *Commentaries on the Constitution.* [131] In addition to signing the Declaration of Independence, McKean was the Chief Justice of the Supreme Court of Pennsylvania. One of the cases over which he presided was *Respublica v. John Roberts.* [132] In that case, John Roberts was sentenced

1792 COMMENTARIES

to death after a jury found him guilty of treason. Chief Justice McKean then delivered a Gospel message to John Roberts in the courtroom, admonishing him to accept Christ before his death, so that he could spend eternity in heaven rather than hell. [133]

SAMUEL ADAMS

There are so many other signers of our Founding documents with manifest Christian declarations. Consider the words of various signers of the Declaration, beginning with Samuel Adams:

> I ... [rely] upon the merits of Jesus Christ for a pardon of all my sins. [134]

CHARLES CARROLL

Charles Carroll similarly declared:

> On the mercy of my Redeemer I rely for salvation and on His merits; not on the works I have done in obedience to His precepts. [135]

JOHN WITHERSPOON

John Witherspoon urged:

> I ... [entreat] you in the most earnest manner to believe in Jesus Christ, for "there is no salvation in any other" [ACTS 4:12]. ... [I]f you are not reconciled to God through Jesus Christ, if you are not clothed with the spotless robe of His righteousness, you must forever perish. [136]

ROBERT PAINE

Robert Treat Paine declared:

> I am constrained to express my adoration of the Supreme Being – the Author of my existence – in full belief of ... His forgiving mercy revealed to the world through Jesus Christ, through Whom I hope for never ending happiness in a future state. [137]

RICHARD STOCKTON

Richard Stockton declared:

> [I] subscribe to the entire belief of the great and leading doctrines of the Christian religion, ... [and I exhort] that the course of life held up in the Christian system is calculated for the most complete happiness that can be enjoyed in this mortal state. [138]

DR. BENJAMIN RUSH

Dr. Benjamin Rush succinctly declared:

> My only hope of salvation is in the infinite tran-
> scendent love of God manifested to the world
> by the death of His Son upon the Cross. Noth-
> ing but His blood will wash away my sins [ACTS
> 22:16]. I rely exclusively upon it. Come, Lord
> Jesus! Come quickly! [REVELATION 22:20] [139]

Consider the words of some of the signers of the
Constitution. John Dickinson declared:

> Rendering thanks to my Creator ... for my birth
> in a country enlightened by the Gospel ... to
> Him I resign myself, humbly confiding in His
> goodness and in His mercy through Jesus Christ
> for the events of eternity. [140]

JOHN DICKINSON

Gunning Bedford declared:

> To the triune God – the Father, the Son, and the
> Holy Ghost – be ascribed all honor and dominion,
> forevermore – Amen. [141]

GUNNING BEDFORD

Roger Sherman (a signer of both the Declaration and the Constitution) declared:

> I believe that there is one only living and
> true God, existing in three persons, the
> Father, the Son, and the Holy Ghost. ...
> [and] that at the end of this world there
> will be a resurrection of the dead and a
> final judgment of all mankind when the
> righteous shall be publicly acquitted by
> Christ the Judge and admitted to ever-
> lasting life and glory, and the wicked be
> sentenced to everlasting punishment. [142]

ROGER SHERMAN

And John Jay, the original Chief Justice of the U. S. Supreme Court and an author of the *Federalist Papers*, declared:

> Unto Him who is the author and giver of all good, I render sincere and humble thanks for His manifold and unmerited blessings, and especially for our redemption and salvation by His beloved Son.... Blessed be His holy name. [143]

JOHN JAY

These Founding Fathers, and the overwhelming majority of the others, were overt Christians and were not enemies of Christ, nor were they atheists – despite what current sources may claim.

To the contrary, God was so important to the Founding Fathers that when they met in Congress for the first time, in September of 1774, they opened with prayer. But apparently it was not a routine, genteel little prayer such as those often prayed at public meetings

THE FIRST PRAYER IN CONGRESS

today. According to the writings of those who were there, that time of prayer in Congress was momentous as well as extended. [144] In fact, John Adams explained that Congress not only prayed but that it also studied four chapters of the Bible – in Congress. That Bible study was so timely, and one chapter in that study had such a profound effect upon the delegates, that John Adams wrote his wife Abigail, telling her:

> I never saw a greater effect upon an audience. It seemed as if Heaven had ordained that Psalm to be read on the morning. . . . I must beg you to read that Psalm. . . . [R]ead this letter and the 35th Psalm to [your friends]. Read it to your father. [145]

JOHN ADAMS WRITING

(Her father was the Rev. William Smith, the pastor of their local church.)

Silas Deane said that this time of prayer and Scripture reading in Congress was so powerful that "even Quakers shed tears." [146]

There is no doubt that America has been a successful nation with a stable, successful government because of the foundation on which it was built – a foundation unlike any other nation in the world. In fact, George Washington, in his famous "Farewell Address" of 1796, reminded Americans why our government and its policies were so successful. He declared:

> Of all the dispositions and habits which lead to political prosperity, religion and morality are indispensable supports. [147]

WASHINGTON PRAYING

Yet many Americans today, including many Christians, have fallen into believing that Christians should not be involved in civil government – that there should be some sort of a compartmentalization – that faith should be kept in one arena, real life in another, and the two should never meet. The Bible does not teach that; and our Founding Fathers and early ministers did not believe that.

Yet many critics today try to invoke what Jesus said in Matthew 22 as proof that Christians should not be involved; but this is a complete mischaracterization of that passage. Matthew 22:21 says that we are to "render unto Caesar the things that are Caesar's, and unto God the things that are God's." But does this mean that God's people are not to be involved with "Caesar"? Why did Jesus make this statement? He was asked whether it was right to pay taxes. In response, Jesus picked up a coin, asked whose inscription was on it, and when they said, "Caesar's," Jesus replied, "Then render to Caesar what is Caesar's, and to God what is God's." That is, render your due to the government, and render your due to God – you have responsibilities in both areas. He clearly was not saying to avoid the governmental arena.

Beyond the passage in Matthew 22, there are many other Biblical passages where God endorses the involvement of His people in the civil arena – an institution that He Himself created and ordained.

For example, in Romans 13:4-6, on three separate occasions, the Scripture declares that those who are in civil government are "ministers of God." (Perhaps this is why so many ministers were involved in the civil arena during the Founding Era – they believed and obeyed the Bible.)

Hebrews 11 is the "Faith Hall of Fame" where the great heroes of our faith are held up to us as examples; in fact, Hebrews 12 declares that it is these heroes who are cheering us on. Yet, notice that the heroes of our faith listed in Hebrews 11:22-34 were involved in civil government. Why would God hold them up to us as examples to emulate if He thought it was wrong for His people to be involved in the civil arena?

In I Timothy 2:1-2, we are told to pray "first of all" for all people – for our leaders and those in authority. Notice: God tells us to pray for our civil leaders "first of all" – before we pray for ourselves, our families, or our churches. There is nothing else in the Bible that God tells us to pray for "first of all." This must mean that God considers civil government important.

Recall the parable of the minas in Luke 19. The Master calls His servants together and gives them all a mina – a trust – a stewardship. The Master departs and then later returns to take account of their stewardship. One had taken the mina and turned it into ten; another had turned his into five; and another had taken his trust and not used it at all. The one who refused to get involved with what the Master had entrusted him was the one who got in trouble; but notice the reward for the other two. To the first, the Master said, "Well done good and faithful servant; I will make you a ruler over ten cities"; to the second he said, "Well done, I will make you a ruler over five cities." Notice the reward of the Master for their faithful stewardship: he places them into civil government! Today, most Christians don't think of being in civil government as a reward from the Master; maybe it is time to rethink our beliefs about civil government based on what the Bible says.

Despite the rich heritage of Christian faith and expression in America and the strong foundation that it has provided for our country, things have begun to change dramatically. Hundreds of years of religious freedoms have been erased by courts in only a few short decades. While there have been scores of horrible rulings, perhaps none is any more egregious than the ruling in a case that went to the U. S. Supreme Court: *Jane Doe v. Santa Fe Independent School District.*

Santa Fe is a small rural town outside of Houston, Texas; it has a long tradition of prayer at graduations and prayer at athletic events such as football games. Yet a handful of students in that school were offended by the practice; they did not want anyone else praying. So they went to a federal judge and asked him to force everyone else to stop praying.

The judge ruled that he would allow prayer to continue at graduations and athletic events – but only if students prayed the right words when they prayed. He warned:

> The Court will allow that prayer to be a typical nondenominational prayer, which can refer to God or the Almighty or that sort of thing. The prayer must not refer to ... Jesus ... or anyone else. And make no mistake, the Court is going to have a United States marshal in attendance at the graduation. If any student offends this Court, that student will be summarily arrested and will face up to six months incarceration in the Galveston County Jail for contempt of Court. ... Anybody who violates

these orders, no kidding, is going to wish that he or she had died as a child when this Court gets through with it. [148]

Died as a child? If you pray the wrong words in a prayer, you are going to wish that you "had died as a child when this court gets through" with you?

This ruling obviously angers most citizens, and the common response is, "What's wrong with this judge? Can't he read the Constitution? The Constitution says nothing about "separation of church and state"; that phrase appears nowhere in the Constitution; it was a policy enacted by the Supreme Court in 1947 in its efforts to compartmentalize faith and segregate it from public life. The Constitution specifically guarantees Americans the 'free exercise of religion'! Can't this judge read the Constitution?"

Sentiments like this reflect a basic misunderstanding. Most citizens believe that the Constitution governs America, but it does not. In fact, while the Founding Fathers were framing the Constitution at the Constitutional Convention, there was a discussion over what the impact of the Constitution would be in limiting the misconduct of public officials. The discussion was best summed up by delegate John Francis Mercer, who declared:

JOHN FRANCIS MERCER

It is a great mistake to suppose that the paper we are to propose will govern the United States. [149]

In other words, it is a major error to believe that the Constitution governs America. He continued:

It is the men whom it will bring into the government and interest [they have] in maintaining it that are to govern them. The paper will only mark out the mode and the form. Men are the substance and must do the business. [150]

In short, the Constitution gives citizens the power to elect leaders; but if the wrong kind of leaders are elected, the Constitution will be absolutely worthless in their hands – as it was in the hands of the judge in Santa Fe, Texas, and so many other judges and elected officials.

This same lesson had been taught in the Scriptures long before it was applied in America: was there any nation in the history of the world that had better civil laws than Israel? Certainly not, for God Almighty had given their laws. Yet, how good were their God-inspired, God-given laws when they had rulers such as Ahab and Jezebel, or Manasseh, or Jeroboam, or Rehoboam, or other wicked leaders? Despite the fact that their laws were from God Himself, those superb laws were completely disregarded under corrupt and deficient leaders.

The Founders understood this, and one of the most frequently quoted Bible principles invoked by the Founders is the one set forth in Proverbs 29:2:

> When the righteous rule, the people rejoice; when the wicked rule, the people groan.

The key to good government is not how good our documents are or how good our laws are; rather it is how good our leaders are. In America, whether the righteous rule, or whether the wicked rule depends totally upon the will of the voters: we have our choice.

In recent years, Christian voters have not taken their voting stewardship seriously. In elections from 1992-2000, Christian voter turnout fell by forty percent. There are sixty million evangelicals in America, and in the 2000 presidential election, only fifteen million voted. In fact, twenty-four million of those sixty million evangelicals were not even registered to vote! [151]

To have been given the power to determine the quality of our government and its leaders, and then not to use that power, is reminiscent of the servant who received a trust from the Master and decided not to do anything with it – not to get involved. None of the servants asked for the trust that they received from the Master; but the Master gave it to them anyway; and they became responsible to the Master for what they did with that trust – despite the fact they had not asked for it. Similarly, we did not ask to be born in America; we did not ask to be given a government of which we are the stewards; nevertheless, the Master has given it to us; and He _will_ call us to account for our stewardship of this important trust.

If our culture is moving the wrong way in America, it is because of Christian non-involvement. James A. Garfield, the 20th President of the United States, pointed this out a century ago.

President Garfield was a minister of the Gospel. In a handwritten letter, he recounts personally preaching the Gospel nineteen times in a revival, with thirty-four people coming to Christ and thirty-one being baptized. [152] Of course, this type of activity and background is not usually associated with our Presidents in the minds of most Americans today, but several of our Presidents were involved in Christian ministry.

A GARFIELD REVIVAL LETTER

Notice what President Garfield reminded Americans a century ago:

Now, more than ever before, the people are responsible for the character of their Congress. If that body be ignorant, reckless, and corrupt, it is because the people tolerate ignorance, recklessness, and corruption. If it be intelligent, brave, and pure, it is because the people demand these high qualities to represent them in the national

JAMES A. GARFIELD

legislature. . . . [I]f the next centennial does not find us a great nation . . . it will be because those who represent the enterprise, the culture, and the morality of the nation do not aid in controlling the political forces. [153]

It is safe to say that we who represent the enterprise, the culture, and the morality of the nation today have done little to control its political forces. Consequently, our national policies do not accurately reflect the values of the nation at large.

For example, 78 percent of the nation supports prayer in schools; [154] 74 percent of the nation wants the Ten Commandments back in the classroom; [155] 68 percent wants creation taught in public schools; [156] 66 percent opposes partial-birth abortions; [157] and there are similarly high numbers in numerous other areas involving faith and values. Yet despite the overwhelming support among the people on these issues, our public policies do not reflect these high numbers. In fact, the support on these issues is not nearly as high in Congress or in the courts as it is in the public. Why? Because Americans who embrace these values simply are not voting, and therefore are not electing to office leaders who embrace those same values.

The Rev. Charles Finney, a leader in America's Second and Third Great Awakenings during the early and mid 1800s, reminded Christians of a lesson we need to remember today:

THE REV. CHARLES FINNEY

The Church must take right ground in regard to politics. . . . [T]he time has come that Christians must vote for honest men and take consistent ground in politics. . . . Christians have been exceedingly guilty in this matter. But the time has come when they must act differently. . . . God cannot sustain this free and blessed country which we love and pray for unless the Church will take right ground. . . . It seems sometimes as if the foundations of the nation are becoming rotten, and Christians seem to act as if they think God does not see what they do in politics. But I tell you He does see it, and He will bless or curse this nation according to the course [Christians] take [in politics]. [158]

What legacy will we leave the next generation? Many Christians argue that the next generation is not our concern – that Christ will return before this. Yet every generation since Christ was on earth has believed that Christ would return in their generation; so far, they have all been wrong. We are told in I Thessalonians 5:2 to expect His return as a "thief in the night," and we should observe that unequivocal admonition. Nevertheless, regardless of what eschatology one might embrace, Jesus has clearly told us all in Luke 19:13 to "occupy until He comes." Therefore, we should heed the warning delivered to citizens in 1803 when the Reverend Matthias Burnet charged:

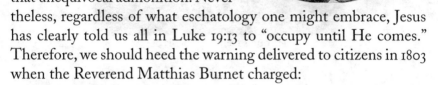

> Finally, ye . . . whose high prerogative it is to . . . invest with office and authority or to withhold them and in whose power it is to save or destroy your country, consider well the important trust . . . which God . . . [has] put into your hands. To God and posterity you are accountable for them [your rights and your rulers]. . . . Let not your children have reason to curse you for giving up those rights and prostrating those institutions which your fathers delivered to you. [159]

It is time for Christians to reengage in civil stewardship from a Biblical viewpoint – a viewpoint long understood by previous generations. It is time for Christians again to become salt and light in every arena of society – including the civil arena – and to influence society through acts as simple as voting. Indeed, the Bible reminds us that "when the righteous rule, the people rejoice"; but the righteous can't rule unless some of the qualified ones are willing to run for office and unless the rest of us are willing to get out and elect them when they do run.

Psalms 33:12 declares that blessed is that nation whose God is the Lord; this nation has been blessed from its beginning, and if America does not stay blessed, it will be because Christians did not stay involved. Get involved – make a positive difference in America again! ■

PLAQUE AT THE U. S. CAPITOL

# Endnotes

1. Lyndon B. Johnson, *Public Papers of Presidents of the United States Containing the Public Messages, Speeches, and Statements of the President* (Washington, DC: Government Printing Office, 1965), Book II: July 1 to December 31, 1964, p. 884, "Remarks Upon Arrival at Andrews Air Force Base," November 22, 1963, quoting President Woodrow Wilson; see also Robert Flood, *The Rebirth of America* (Philadelphia: Arthur S. DeMoss Foundation, 1986), p.12.

2. Charles Beard, *The Economic Basis of Politics* (New York: Alfred A. Knopf, 1945).

3. Peter Thacher, *Brief Account of the Society for Propagating the Gospel Among the Indians and Others in North America* (Boston: 1798), p. 2.

4. Thacher, *Brief Account*, p. 2.

5. Kate Mason Rowland, *The Life of Charles Carroll of Carrollton* (New York: G. P. Putnam's Sons, 1898), Vol. II, pp. 357-358, to John Stanford, October 9, 1827; William V. Wells, *The Life and Public Services of Samuel Adams* (Boston: Little, Brown, and Company, 1865), Vol. I, pp. 502-505, "Natural Rights of the Colonists as Men; The Rights of the Colonists as Christians."

6. Thomas F. Gordon, *The History of Pennsylvania from its Discovery by Europeans to the Declaration of Independence in 1776* (Philadelphia: Carey, Lea & Carey, 1829), pp. 554-555.

7. See, for example, <u>Virginia</u>: Benjamin Franklin, *The Works of Benjamin Franklin*, Jared Sparks, editor (Boston: Tappan, Whittemore, and Mason, 1839), Vol. VIII, p. 42, to Dean Woodward, April 10, 1773; Benson J. Lossing, *Harpers' Popular Cyclopaedia of United States History* (New York: Harper and Brothers, 1892), p. 1299; <u>Massachusetts</u>: W. O. Blake, *The History of Slavery and the Slave Trade* (Columbus: J. & H. Miller, 1858), p. 178; <u>Rhode Island and Connecticut</u>: George M. Stroud, *A Sketch of the Laws Relating to Slavery in the Several States of the United States of America* (Philadelphia: Kimber and Sharpless, 1827), p. 137.

8. Lossing, *Harpers' Popular Cyclopaedia*, pp. 1299-1300; Blake, *History of Slavery*, p. 177; Franklin, *Works*, Vol. VIII, p. 42, to Dean Woodward, April 10, 1773.

9. Frank Moore, *Materials for History Printed From Original Manuscripts, the Correspondence of Henry Laurens of South Carolina* (New York: Zenger Club, 1861), p. 20, to John Laurens, August 14, 1776.

10. Thomas Jefferson, *The Writings of Thomas Jefferson*, Albert Ellery Bergh, editor (Washington, DC: Thomas Jefferson Memorial Assoc., 1903), Vol. I, p. 34.

11. *An Abridgement of the Laws of Pennsylvania*, Collinson Read, editor (Philadelphia: Printed for the Author, 1801), pp. 264-266, Act of March 1, 1780.

12. *A Constitution or Frame of Government Agreed Upon by the Delegates of the People of the State of Massachusetts-Bay* (Boston: Benjamin Edes and Sons, 1780), p. 7, Article I, "Declaration of Rights."

13. *The Public Statute Laws of the State of Connecticut* (Hartford: Hudson and Goodwin, 1808), Book I, pp. 623-625, Act passed in October 1777.

14. *Rhode Island Session Laws* (Providence: Wheeler, 1784), pp. 7-8, Act passed on February 27, 1784.

15. *The Constitutions of the Sixteen States* (Boston: Manning and Loring, 1797), p. 249, Vermont, 1786, Article I, "Declaration of Rights."

16. *The Constitutions of the Sixteen States* (Boston: Manning and Loring, 1797), p. 50, New Hampshire, 1792, Article I, "Bill of Rights."

17. *Laws of the State of New York, Passed at the Twenty-Second Session, Second Meeting of the Legislature* (Albany: Loring Andrew, 1798), pp. 721-723, Act passed on March 29, 1799.

18. Julian P. Boyd, *The Declaration of Independence, the Evolution of the Text as Shown in Facsimiles of Various Drafts by its Author, Thomas Jefferson* (Princeton: Princeton University Press, 1945), pp. 20-21, 31-32, 37.

19. *The Constitution of the Pennsylvania Society for Promoting the Abolition of Slavery, and the Relief of Negroes, Unlawfully held in Bondage* (Philadelphia: Joseph James, 1787), p. 8.

20. To document his anti-slavery work across the decades, see, for example, Benjamin Rush, *The Letters of Benjamin Rush*, L. H. Butterfield, editor (Princeton: Princeton University Press, 1951), Vol. I, pp. 80-81,to Granville Sharp, May 1, 1773; p. 76, to Barbeu Dubourg, April 29, 1773; *Dictionary of American Biography*, s.v. "Benjamin Rush"; *Constitution of the Pennsylvania Society for Promoting the Abolition of Slavery*, p. 8; Rush *Letters*, Vol. II, pp. 754-755, "To the President of the Pennsylvania Abolition Society," 1794; *Minutes of the Proceedings of a Convention of Delegates from the Abolition Societies Established in different Parts of the United States, Assembled at Philadelphia* (Philadelphia: Zachariah Poulson, 1794), pp. 6, 10-11; *Minutes of the Proceedings of the Third Convention of Delegates from the Abolition Societies Established in different Parts of the United States, Assembled at Philadelphia* (Philadelphia: Zachariah Poulson, 1796), p. 8; *Minutes of the Proceedings of the Fourth Convention of Delegates from the Abolition Societies Established in Different Parts of the United States, Assembled at Philadelphia* (Philadelphia: Zachariah Poulson, 1797), p. 12; William Straughton, *An Eulogium in Memory of the Late Dr. Benjamin Rush* (Philadelphia: University of Pennsylvania, 1813), p. 30; *Minutes of the Proceedings of the Thirteenth American Convention for Promoting the Abolition of Slavery and Improving the Condition of the African Race* (Hamilton Ville: John Bouvier, 1812), p. 15.

21. *Minutes of the Proceedings of the Second Convention of Delegates from the Abolition Societies Established in different Parts of the United States, Assembled at Philadelphia* (Philadelphia: Zachariah Poulson, 1795), p. 6, where Dr. Rush was elected national president.

22. Francis Russell, *Adams: An American Dynasty* (New York: American Heritage Publishing, 1976), p. 224.

23. John Quincy Adams, *An Oration Delivered Before the Inhabitants of the Town of Newburyport at their Request on the Sixty-First Anniversary of the Declaration of Independence, July 4, 1837* (Newburyport: Charles Whipple, 1837).

24. John Quincy Adams, *Oration at Newburyport*, pp. 54-60.

25. Wells, *Public Services of Samuel Adams*, Vol. II, p. 412.

26. John Adams, *The Works of John Adams*, Charles Francis Adams, editor (Boston: Little, Brown and Company, 1856), Vol. X, p. 284, to Hezekiah Niles, February 13, 1818.

27. Daniel Dorchester, *Christianity in the United States* (New York: Hunt and Eaton, 1890), pp. 264-265.

28. John Wingate Thornton, *Pulpit of the American Revolution* (Boston: Gould and Lincoln, 1860).

29. *The Patriot Preachers of the American Revolution, With Biographical Sketches, 1766-1783* (Printed for the Subscribers, 1860).

30. J. T. Headley, *The Chaplains and Clergy of the Revolution* (Massachusetts: G. & F. Bill, 1861).

31. Jonathan Mayhew, *A Discourse on Rev. XV. 3d, 4th. Occasioned by the Earthquakes in November 1755* (Boston: Edes & Gill, 1755).

32. Jonathan Mayhew, *A Sermon Occasioned by the Great Fire in Boston, New England, Thursday March 20, 1760* (Boston: Edes and Gill, 1760).

33. Joseph Lathrop, *A Sermon Containing Reflections on the Solar Eclipse, which Appeared on June 16, 1806* (Springfield, MA: Henry Brewer, 1806).

34. Rev. S. C. Aiken, *Moral View of Railroads, A Discourse Delivered on Sabbath Morning, February 23, 1851* (Cleveland: Harris, Fairbanks, and Co., 1851).

35. Joseph Lathrop, *The Infirmities and Comforts of Old Age, A Sermon to Aged People* (Springfield, MA: Henry Brewer, 1805).

36. Nathaniel Fisher, *A Sermon Delivered At Salem, January 14, 1796, Occasioned by the Execution of Henry Blackburn, on that Day, for the Murder of George Wilkinson* (Boston: S. Hall, 1796).

37. Jedediah Morse, *A Sermon, Delivered Before the Ancient & Honorable Artillery Company, in Boston, June 6, 1803, Being the Anniversary of Their Election of Officers* (Charlestown, MA: Samuel Etheridge, 1803).

38. Joseph McKeen, *A Sermon Preached Before the Honorable the Council, and the Honorable the Senate, and House of Representatives of the Commonwealth of Massachusetts, May 28, 1800. Being the Day of General Election* (Boston: Young & Minns, 1800).

39. George Bancroft, *The History of the United States of America, from the Discovery of the Continent* (Boston: Little, Brown and Company, 1858), Vol. I, p. 364.

40. Daniel Foster, *A Sermon Preached Before His Excellency John Hancock, Esq. Governor; His Honor Samuel Adams, Esq. Lieutenant-Governor; The Honorable the Council, Senate, and House of Representatives, of the Commonwealth of Massachusetts, May 26, 1790. Being the Day of General Election* (Boston: Thomas Adams, 1790).

41. Timothy Stone, *A Sermon Preached Before His Excellency Samuel Huntington, Esq. L. L. D. Governor, and the Honorable the General Assembly of the State of Connecticut, Convened at Hartford, on the Day of the Anniversary Election. May 10, 1792* (Hartford: Hudson and Goodwin, 1792).

42. Thomas Baldwin, *A Sermon Delivered Before His Excellency Caleb Strong, Esq. Governor, the Honorable the Council, Senate, and House of Representatives of the Commonwealth of Massachusetts, May 26, 1802. Being the Day of General Election* (Boston: Young & Minns, 1802).

43. John Marsh, *A Sermon Preached before His Honor Oliver Wolcott, Esq. L. L. D. Lieutenant-Governor and Commander in Chief, and the Honorable the General Assembly of the State of Connecticut, Convened at Hartford, on the Day of the Anniversary Election, May 12th, 1796* (Hartford: Hudson and Goodwin, 1796).

44. John Mitchell Mason, *The Voice of Warning to Christians, on the Ensuing Election of a President of the United States* (New York: G. F. Hopkins, 1800).

45. Thomas Jefferson, *The Works of Thomas Jefferson,* Paul Leicester Ford, editor (New York: G. P. Putnams Sons, 1905), Vol. IX, p. 143, to Jeremiah Moor, August 14, 1800.

46. Background information supporting H. R. 2357, "House of Worship Political Speech Protection Act," introduced by Rep. Walter Jones (NC) in the 107th Congress, 2nd Session, 2002.

47. Conseil Constitutionnel, "Les Constitutions de la France" (at http://www.conseil-constitutionnel.fr/textes/constitu.htm); see also Harvard Law School, "French Legal Research: Constitution" (at http://www.law.harvard.edu/library/services/research/guides/international/france/const.php).

48. ICL-Brazil Index, "Constitutional Background" (at http://www.oefre.unibe.ch/law/icl/br__indx.html); see also Georgetown University, "Political Database of the Americas: Federative Republic of Brazil" (at http://pdba.georgetown.edu/Constitutions/Brazil/brazil.html).

49. University of Michigan, "Polskie Konstytucje – Spis Tresci" (at http://www-personal. engin.umich.edu/~zbigniew/Constitutions/index.html).

50. Afghanistan Online, "History" (at http://www.afghan-web.com/history/).

51. Bucknell University, "The History of the Russian Law Codes" (at http://www.departments.bucknell.edu/russian/politics.html).

52. John Adams, *Works*, Vol. X, p. 311, to William Tudor, April 5, 1818.

53. John Adams, *Works*, Vol. X, p. 311, to William Tudor, April 5, 1818; see also Vol. IV, pp. 82-83, "Novanglus," circa 1775; Vol. I, pp. 53-54, to Jonathan Sewell, February 1760; Benjamin Franklin, *The Papers of Benjamin Franklin*, William B. Willcox, editor (New Haven: Yale University Press, 1973), Vol. 17, p. 6, "The Colonist's Advocate," January 4, 1770; Vol. 4, p. 107, "Idea of the English School"; Thomas Jefferson, *Writings*, Vol. VIII, p. 31, to Thomas Mann Randolph, May 30, 1790; Vol. XI, p. 222, to John Norvell, June 11, 1807; Benjamin Rush, *The Selected Writings of Benjamin Rush*, Dagobert D. Runes, editor (New York: Philosophical Library, Inc., 1947), p. 78, "Observations on the Government of Pennsylvania"; Benjamin Rush, *Medical Inquiries and Observations* (Philadelphia: Thomas Dobson, 1794), Vol. I, p. 332, "Duties of a Physician"; Benjamin Rush, *Three Lectures Upon Animal Life, Delivered in the University of Pennsylvania* (Philadelphia: Budd and Bartram, 1799), p. 23; Benjamin Rush, *Medical Inquiries and Observations* (Philadelphia: J. Conrad & Co., 1805), Vol. II, p. 19, "The Influence of Physical Causes Upon the Moral Faculty."

54. John Quincy Adams, *The Jubilee of the Constitution* (New York: Samuel Colman, 1839), p. 40.

55. See, for example, *Concise Oxford Dictionary of World Religions*, John Bowker, editor (Oxford: Oxford University Press, 2000), p. 151; Franklin L. Baumer, *Religion and the Use of Skepticism* (New York: Harcourt, Brace, & Company, 1960), pp. 57-59; James A. Herrick, *The Radical Rhetoric of the English Deists: The Discourse of Skepticism, 1680-1750* (Columbia, SC: University of South Carolina Press, 1997), p. 15; Kerry S. Walters, *Rational Infidels: The American Deists* (Durango, CO: Longwood Academic, 1992), pp. 24, 210; Kerry S. Walters, *The American Deists: Voices of Reason and Dissent in the Early Republic* (Lawrence, KS: University Press of Kansas, 1992), pp. 6-7; John W. Yolton, *John Locke and the Way of Ideas* (Oxford: Oxford University Press, 1956), pp. 25, 115.

56. See Richard Watson, *Theological Institutes: Or a View of the Evidences, Doctrines, Morals, and Institutions of Christianity* (New York: Carlton and Porter, 1857), Vol. I, p. 5, where Watson includes John Locke as a theologian.

57. *Encyclopedia Britannica*, Eleventh Edition, 1911, *s.v.* "John Locke."

58. Jefferson, *Writings*, Vol. XV, p. 462, to James Madison, August 30, 1823.

59. Donald S. Lutz, "The Relative Influence of European Writers on Late Eighteenth Century American Political Thought," *American Political Science Review*, Vol. 78, Issue 1, March 1984, p. 191.

60. Lutz, "Relative Influence," pp. 191-193; see also Donald Lutz, *The Origins of American Constitutionalism* (Baton Rouge: Louisiana State University Press, 1988), pp. 141-142.

61. George Washington, *Address of George Washington, President of the United States, and Late Commander in Chief of the American Army, to the People of the United States, Preparatory to His Declination* (Baltimore: George and Henry S. Keatinge, 1796), p. 22; *The Federalist*, #15 by Alexander Hamilton.

62. Noah Webster, *Letters to a Young Gentleman Commencing His Education* (New Haven: S. Converse, 1823), pp. 18-19, Letter 1; see also a similar comment in Noah Webster, *His-*

*tory of the United States* (New Haven: Durrie & Peck, 1832), pp. 336-337, ¶49, although the Scripture citation in this work is closer to 2 Samuel 23:3 than Exodus 18:21.

63. William Jay, *The Life of John Jay* (New York: J. & J. Harper, 1833), Vol. II, p. 376, to John Murray, Jr., October 12, 1816; George Washington, *The Writings of George Washington*, Jared Sparks, editor (Boston: Russell, Odiorne, and Metcalf; and Hilliard, Gray, and Co., 1835), Vol. IX, pp. 391-392, to Benjamin Lincoln, June 29, 1788.

64. John Adams, *Works*, Vol. X, p. 45, to Thomas Jefferson, June 28, 1813.

65. Elias Boudinot, *The Life, Public Services, Addresses, and Letters of Elias Boudinot*, J. J. Boudinot, editor (Boston: Houghton, Mifflin and Co., 1896), Vol. I, pp. 19, 21, speech in the First Provincial Congress of New Jersey.

66. Bernard C. Steiner, *The Life and Correspondence of James McHenry* (Cleveland: Burrows Brothers, 1907), p. 475, Charles Carroll to James McHenry, November 4, 1800.

67. *Independent Chronicle* (Boston), November 2, 1780, last page; see also Abram English Brown, *John Hancock, His Book* (Boston: Lee and Shepard, 1898), p. 269.

68. Benjamin Rush, *Essays, Literary, Moral and Philosophical* (Philadelphia: Thomas and Samuel F. Bradford, 1798), p. 8, "Of the Mode of Education Proper in a Republic"; see also Rush, *Letters*, Vol. II, pp. 820-821, to Thomas Jefferson, August 22, 1800, and Rush, *Essays*, pp. 112-113, "Defense of the Use of the Bible as a School Book."

69. Stephen Hopkins, *The Rights of Colonies Examined* (Providence: William Goddard, 1765), pp. 23-24.

70. Wells, *Public Services of Samuel Adams*, Vol. III, pp. 372-373, to Thomas Paine, November 30, 1802; see also Vol. I, p. 504; Samuel Adams and John Adams, *Four Letters: Being an Interesting Correspondence Between Those Eminently Distinguished Characters, John Adams, Late President of the United States; and Samuel Adams, Late Governor of Massachusetts. On the Important Subject of Government* (Boston: Adams and Rhoades, 1802), pp. 9-10.

71. Washington, *Writings*, Vol. XV, p. 55, speech to the Delaware Indian Chiefs, May 12, 1779; see also Washington, *Writings*, Vol. V, pp. 244-245, July 9, 1776 (this statement of George Washington was also used by Abraham Lincoln in his November 15, 1862, order to his troops to maintain regular Sabbath observances; see Abraham Lincoln, *Letters and Addresses of Abraham Lincoln*, Mary MacLean, editor (New York: Unit Book Publishing Co., 1907), p. 261); see also Washington, *Writings*, Vol. II, pp. 342-343, General Orders, May 2, 1778.

72. Alexander Hamilton, *The Papers of Alexander Hamilton*, Harold C. Syrett, editor (New York: Columbia University Press, 1977), Vol. XXV, pp. 605-610, to James Bayard, April 16-21, 1802.

73. *Reports of the Proceedings and Debates of the Convention of 1821, Assembled for the Purpose of Amending The Constitution of the State of New York* (Albany: E. and E. Hosford, 1821), p. 575, Rufus King, October 30, 1821.

74. John Dickinson, *The Political Writings of John Dickinson* (Wilmington: Bonsal and Niles, 1801), Vol. I, p. 111.

75. *The Debates and Proceedings in the Congress of the United States* (Washington, DC: Gales and Seaton: 1834), Vol. I, pp. 949-950, September 25, 1789.

76. *M'Creery's Lessee v. Allender*, 4 Harris & McHenry 258, 259 (Sup. Ct. Md. 1799), where Justice Samuel Chase applied a belief in Christianity as the basis of citizenship in this case.

77. Jay, *Life of John Jay*, Vol. II, p. 376, to John Murray, Jr., October 12, 1816.

78. Joseph Story, *A Familiar Exposition of the Constitution of the United States* (New York: Harper & Brothers, 1854), pp. 259, 261, §441, 444; see also Joseph Story, *Commentaries on*

*the Constitution of the United States* (Boston: Hilliard, Gray, and Company, 1833), Vol. III, p. 726, §1868; Joseph Story, *Life and Letters of Joseph Story*, William W. Story, editor (Boston: Charles C. Little and James Brown, 1851), Vol. II, p. 8.

79. *People v. Ruggles*, 8 Johns 545, 545-547 (Sup. Ct. NY. 1811).

80. Zephaniah Swift, *A System of Laws of the State of Connecticut* (Windham, CT: John Byrne, 1796), Vol. II, pp. 323-324.

81. *Dictionary of American Biography, s.v.* "Zephaniah Swift."

82. *Church of the Holy Trinity v. U. S.*, 143 U. S. 457, 465, 470-471 (1892); *Vidal v. Girard's Executors,* 43 U. S. 126, 198 (1844); *Davis v. Beason*, 133 U. S. 333, 341-344, 348 n. (1890); *United States v. Macintosh*, 283 U. S. 605, 625 (1931).

83. *Reports of Committee the House of Representatives Made During the First Session of the Thirty-Third Congress* (Washington, DC: A. O. P. Nicholson, 1854), pp. 8-9; and *The Reports of the Committees of the Senate of the United States For the Second Session of the Thirty-Second Congress* (Washington, DC: Robert Armstrong, 1853), p. 3.

84. See *Updegraph v. The Commonwealth*, 11 S. & R. 394, 399 (Sup. Ct. Pa. 1824); *People v. Ruggles*, 8 Johns. 290, 293, 296 (Sup. Ct. NY 1811); *M'Creery's Lessee v. Allender*, 4 Harris & McHenry 256, 259 (Sup. Ct. Md. 1799); *Runkel v. Winemiller*, 4 Harris & McHenry 276, 288 (Sup. Ct. Md. 1799); *City Council of Charleston v. S. A. Benjamin*, 2 Strob. 508, 518-521 (Sup. Ct. S.C. 1846); *Lindenmuller v. The People*, 33 Barb 548, 560-564, 567 (Sup. Ct. NY 1861); *Shover v. State*, 10 English 259, 263 (Sup. Ct. Ark. 1850); *Commonwealth v. Nesbit*, 84 Pa. 398, 406-407, 411 (Sup. Ct. Pa. 1859); and many others.

85. Charles Prentiss, *The Life of the Late Gen. William Eaton* (Brookfield, MA: Merriam & Company, 1813), pp. 92-93, to Timothy Pickering, June 15, 1799; p. 146, to Mr. Smith, June 27, 1800; p. 150, to Timothy Pickering, July 4, 1800; p. 185, to John Marshall, September 2, 1800; p. 325, from Eaton's journal, April 8, 1805; and p. 334, from Eaton's journal, May 23, 1805.

86. Daniel Webster, *Mr. Webster's Speech in Defence of the Christian Ministry and in Favor of the Religious Instruction of the Young. Delivered in the Supreme Court of the United States, February 10, 1844, in the Case of Stephen Girard's Will* (Washington, DC: Gales and Seaton, 1844), pp. 41, 43, 50, 51, *passim.*

87. John Quincy Adams, *Oration at Newburyport*, pp. 5-6; see also John Quincy Adams, *An Address Delivered at the Request of the Committee of Arrangements for the Celebrating the Anniversary of Independence at the City of Washington on the Fourth of July 1821* (Cambridge: Hilliard and Metcalf, 1821), p. 28.

88. Abraham Lincoln, *The Works of Abraham Lincoln: Speeches and Debates*, John H. Clifford, editor (New York: University Society Inc., 1908), Vol. III, pp. 126-127, speech of August 17, 1858.

89. Woodrow Wilson, *The Papers of Woodrow Wilson*, Arthur S. Link, editor (Princeton: Princeton University Press, 1977), Vol. 23, p. 20, An Address in Denver on the Bible, May 7, 1911, in which President Wilson declared, "America was born a Christian nation. America was born to exemplify that devotion to the elements of righteousness which are derived from the revelations of Holy Scripture."

90. *Zachary Taylor, 1784-1850; Millard Fillmore, 1800-1874: Chronology Documents Bibliographical Aids,* John J. Farrell, editor (Dobbs Ferry, NY: Oceana Publications, Inc., 1971), p. 27, Inaugural Address, March 5, 1849, in which President Zachary Taylor declared, "I congratulate you, my fellow-citizens, upon the high state of prosperity to which the goodness of Divine Providence has conducted our common country. Let us invoke a continuance of the same

protecting care which has led us from small beginnings to the eminence we this day occupy;" Stephen Abbott Northrop, *A Cloud of Witnesses* (Portland: American Heritage Ministries, 1987, reprinted from the 1894 work), pp. 447-448, in which President Taylor, upon receiving a Bible, declared, "I accept with gratitude and pleasure your gift of this inestimable Volume. It was for the love of the truths of this great Book that our fathers abandoned their native shores for the wilderness. Animated by its lofty principles they toiled and suffered till the desert blossomed as the rose. The same truths sustained them in their resolutions to become a free nation; and guided by the wisdom of this Book they founded a government under which we have grown from three millions to more than twenty millions of people, and from being but a stock on the borders of this Continent we have spread from the Atlantic to the Pacific."

91. Harry S. Truman, *Public Papers of the Presidents of the United States Harry S. Truman Containing the Public Messages, Speeches, and Statements of the President* (Washington, DC: Government Printing Office, 1962), January 1 to December 31, 1946, p. 512, "Address at the Lighting of the National Community Christmas Tree on the White House Grounds," December 24, 1946, in which President Truman declared, "In this great country of ours has been demonstrated the fundamental unity of Christianity and democracy."; see also the volume for January 1 to December 31, 1947, p. 424, "Exchange of Messages with Pope Pius XII," August 28, 1947, in which President Truman declared, "Your holiness, this is a Christian Nation. More than a half century ago that declaration was written into the decrees of the highest court in this land. It is not without significance that the valiant pioneers who left Europe to establish settlements here, at the very beginning of their colonial enterprises declared their faith in the Christian religion and made ample provision for its practice and for its support."; see also the volume for January 1 to December 31, 1949, pp. 582-583, "Address at the Unveiling of a Memorial Carillon in Arlington National Cemetery," December 21, 1949, in which President Truman declared, "Our American heritage of human freedom is born of the belief that man is created in the image of God and therefore is capable of governing himself. We have created here a government dedicated to the dignity and the freedom of man. It is a government whose creed is derived from the word of God, and its roots are deep in our spiritual foundations. Our democracy is an expression of faith in the spirit of man, and it is a declaration of faith in man as created by God. On these spiritual foundations we have established a creed of self-government more precious to us than life itself."; see also the volume for January 1 to December 31, 1950, p. 157, "Address Before the Attorney General's conference on Law Enforcement Problems," February 15, 1950, in which President Truman declared, "The fundamental basis of this Nation's law was given to Moses on the Mount. The fundamental basis of our Bill of Rights comes from the teachings which we get from Exodus and St. Matthew, from Isaiah and St. Paul. I don't think we emphasize that enough these days."

92. *Andrew Jackson 1767-1845: Chronology, Documents, Bibliographical Aids*, Ronald E. Shaw, editor (Dobbs Ferry, NY: Oceana Publications, Inc., 1969), p. 22, "First Inaugural Address," March 4, 1829, in which President Jackson declared, "And a firm reliance on the goodness of that Power whose providence mercifully protected our national infancy, and has since upheld our liberties in various vicissitudes, encourages me to offer up my ardent supplications that He will continue to make our beloved country the object of His divine care and gracious benediction."; p. 70, "The Proclamation to the People of South Carolina," December 10 1832, in which President Jackson declared, "May the Great Ruler of Nations grant that the signal blessings with which He has favored ours may not, by the madness of party or personal ambition, be disregarded and lost; and may His wise providence bring

those who have produced this crises to see the folly before they feel the misery of civil strife, and inspire a returning veneration for the Union which, if we may dare to penetrate His designs, He has chose as the only means of attaining the high destinies to which we may reasonably aspire."; p. 73, "Second Inaugural Address," March 4, 1833, in which President Jackson declared, "Finally, it is my most fervent prayer to that Almighty Being before whom I now stand, and who has kept us in His hands from the infancy of our Republic to the present day, that He will so overrule all my intentions and actions and inspire the hearts of my fellow citizens that we may be preserved from dangers of all kinds and continue forever a united and happy people."; Andrew Jackson, *Memoirs of General Andrew Jackson, Seventh President of the United States* (Auburn, NY: James C. Derby & Co., 1845), p. 240, "President Jackson's Farewell Address," in which President Jackson declared, "Providence has showered on this favored land blessings without number, and has chosen you as the guardians of freedom, to preserve it for the benefits of the human race. May He, who holds in his hands the destinies of nations, make you worthy of the favors He has bestowed, and enable you, with pure hearts, and pure hands, and sleepless vigilance, to guard and defend to the end of time the great charge he has committed to your keeping."; Ronald Reagan, *Public Papers of the Presidents of the United States, Ronald Reagan Containing the Public Messages, Speeches, and Statements of the President* (Washington, DC: Government Printing Office, 1983), January 1 to December 31, 1983, p. 180, Proclamation 5018 in 1983, "The Year of the Bible," citing from Andrew Jackson's declaration that the Bible "is the rock on which our Republic rests"; see the same quote in a proclamation from President George H. W. Bush on February 22, 1990, "International Year of Bible Reading," in *Code of Federal Regulations* (Washington, DC: Government Printing Office, 1991), p. 21.

93. *A Compilation of Messages and Papers of the Presidents:* (New York: Bureau of National Literature, Inc., 1897), p. 6292, Executive Mansion, April 11, 1898, to the Congress of the United States, in which President McKinley declared, "If this measure attains a successful result, then our aspirations as a Christian, peace-loving people will be realized."

94. Herbert Hoover, *Public Papers of the Presidents of the United States, Herbert Hoover Containing the Public Messages, Speeches, and Statements of the President* (Washington, DC: Government Printing Office, 1976), January 1 to December 31, 1931, p. 490, "Radio Address to the Nation on Unemployment Relief," October 18, 1931, in which President Hoover declares, "American life is builded and can alone survive upon the translation into individual action of the fundamental philosophy announced by the Savior nineteen centuries ago."

95. Theodore Roosevelt, *American Ideals, The Strenuous Life, Realizable Ideals* (New York: Charles Scribner's Sons, 1926), pp. 498-499, "We ask that these associations, and the men and women who take part in them, practise the Christian doctrines which are preached from every true pulpit. The Decalogue and the Golden Rule must stand as the foundation of every successful effort to better either our social or our political life. 'Fear the Lord and walk in his ways' and 'Love thy neighbor as thyself' – when we practice these two precepts, the reign of social and civic righteousness will be close at hand. Christianity teaches not only that each of us must so live as to save his own soul, but that each must also strive to do his whole duty by his neighbor. We cannot live up to these teachings as we should; for in the presence of infinite might and infinite wisdom, the strength of the strongest man is but weakness, and the keenest of mortal eyes see but dimly. But each of us can at least strive, as light and strength are given him, toward the ideal. Effort along any one line will not suffice. We must not only be good, but strong. We must not only be high-minded, but brave-hearted. We must think

loftily and we must also work hard. It is not written in the Holy Book that we must merely be harmless as doves. It is also written that we must be wise as serpents. Craft unaccompanied by conscience makes the crafty man a social wild beast who preys on the community and must be hunted out of it. Gentleness and sweetness unbacked by strength and high resolve are almost impotent for good. The true Christian is the true citizen."

96. Noah Webster, *History*, pp. v, 299-300, ¶578; *see also* Noah Webster, *A Collection of Papers on Political, Literary, and Moral Subjects* (New York: Webster and Clark, 1843), pp. 291-292, "Reply to a Letter of David McClure on the Subject of the Proper Course of Study in the Girard College," October 25, 1836.

97. Jedediah Morse, *A Sermon Exhibiting the Present Danger, and Consequent Duties of the Citizens of the United States of America. Delivered at Charlestown, April 25, 1799* (Hartford: Hudson and Goodwin, 1799), p. 9.

98. William H. McGuffey, *McGuffey's Eclectic Fourth Reader* (Cincinnati: Winthrop B. Smith & Co., 1849), p. 9, preface.

99. Thomas Jefferson, *Notes on the State of Virginia* (Philadelphia: Matthew Carey, 1794), Query XVII, pp. 233-234.

100. Hugh A. Garland, *The Life of John Randolph of Roanoke* (New York: D. Appleton & Co., 1853), p. 102, to Dr. Brockenbrough, September 25, 1818.

101. Garland, *Life of John Randolph*, pp. 87-88, from Francis Scott Key, May-June 1816; pp. 99-100, to Francis Scott Key, September 7, 1818; pp. 103-104, from Francis Scott Key; pp. 106-107, Key's reply to Randolph's letter of May 3, 1819; pp. 108-109, Key's reply to Randolph's letter of August 8, 1819.

102. Garland, *Life of John Randolph*, pp. 99-100, to Francis Scott Key, September 7, 1818; pp. 100-102, to Dr. Brockenbrough, September 25, 1818; p. 106, to Francis Scott Key, May 3, 1819; pp. 107-109, to Francis Scott Key, August 22, 1819; pp. 373-374.

103. Rush, *Essays*, p. 8, "Of the Mode of Education Proper in a Republic."

104. Rush, *Letters*, Vol. I, p. 474, to Elias Boudinot, July 9, 1788.

105. From the will of Elias Boudinot available from the New Jersey State Archives; see also George Adams Boyd, *Elias Boudinot: Patriot and Statesman* (Princeton: Princeton University Press, 1952), p. 261.

106. *Reports of Committees of the House of Representatives*, pp. 6, 8-9.

107. *Church of the Holy Trinity v. U. S.*, 143 U. S. 457, 470-471 (1892).

108. William Edelen, "Our Founding presidents were not Christians," *Santa Barbara News-Press*, February 4, 2001, G-5.

109. Steven Morris, "The Founding Fathers Were *Not* Christians," *Free Inquiry*, Fall 1995, p. 12.

110. Rob Massey, "Authors of the Declaration were Enemies of Christ," *Sun Herald*, July 3, 1999, editorial.

111. Steven Morris, "America's Unchristian Beginnings," *The Los Angeles Times*, August 3, 1995, p. B-9. This article was picked up on national wire services and appeared in newspapers across the nation.

112. Isaac Kramnick, R. Laurence Moore, *The Godless Constitution, The Case Against Religious Correctness* (New York: W. W. Norton & Company, 1996).

113. Franklin, *Papers*, Vol. 3, pp. 226-227, n, Proclamation for a General Fast on December 9, 1747; see also Franklin, *Works* (1840), Vol. I, pp. 148-149.

114. Benjamin Franklin, *Proposals Relating to the Education of Youth in Pennsylvania* (Philadelphia, 1749), p. 22.

115. Jared Sparks, *Life of Benjamin Franklin, Containing the Autobiography, with Notes* (Boston: Tappan and Dennet, 1844), p. 352; *see also* Franklin, *Works*, Vol. X, pp. 208-209, n, to Granville Sharp, July 5, 1785.

116. Franklin, *Papers*, Vol. 6, p. 469, to George Whitefield, July 2, 1756.

117. Franklin, *Works*, Vol. X, pp. 281-282, to Thomas Paine in 1790.

118. James Madison, *The Papers of James Madison*, Henry D. Gilpin, editor (Washington, DC: Langtree and O'Sullivan, 1840), Vol. II, pp. 984-986, Franklin's speech of June 28, 1787.

119. Thomas Jefferson, *The Papers of Thomas Jefferson*, Julian P. Boyd, editor (Princeton: Princeton University Press, 1950), Vol. I, pp. 494-497, "Report on a Seal for the United States, with Related Papers," August 20, 1776.

120. *American State Papers: Documents, Legislative, and Executive of the Congress of the United States*, Walter Lowrie and Matthew St. Claire Clark, editors (Washington, DC: Gales and Seaton, 1832), Vol. V, Indian Affairs, Vol. I, p. 687, "The Kaskaskia and Other Tribes"; *see also American Mercury*, March 1, 1804, p. 2, "A Treaty Between the United States of America and the Kaskaskia Tribe of Indians."

121. See, for example, his presidential letter of October 18, 1804 (from an original document in our possession).

122. See John Sergeant, *Eulogy on Charles Carroll of Carrollton Delivered at the Request of the Select and Common Councils of the City of Philadelphia, December 31, 1832* (Philadelphia: Lydia R. Bailey, 1833), p. 18. In that day, all major American colleges existed primarily for religious training or the training of ministers and were thus called "seminaries" of learning. (For example, according to John Sergeant – an attorney and a Member of Congress – 29 of the signers of the Declaration "received their education at . . . public seminaries.") In fact, according to the documents of America's major colleges, Harvard's motto was "For Christ and the Church"; William & Mary existed so that "youth may be piously enacted in good letters and manners and that the Christian faith may be propagated"; Yale told its students, "the great end of all your studies . . . is to obtain the clearest conceptions of Divine things and to lead you to a saving knowledge of God in his Son Jesus Christ"; Princeton required that "every student shall attend worship in the college hall morning and evening"; Dartmouth declared that it was established "for the education and instruction of youths . . . in reading, writing, and all parts of learning which shall appear necessary and expedient for civilizing and Christianizing the children"; Columbia College declared that "no candidate shall be admitted into the College . . . unless he shall be able to render into English . . . the Gospels from the Greek"; etc. Signers of the Declaration attending schools that emphasized a religious course of instruction included John Adams, Samuel Adams, John Hancock, Robert Treat Paine, Elbridge Gerry, William Ellery, William Williams, and William Hooper from Harvard; Oliver Wolcott, Philip Livingston, Lewis Morris, and Lyman Hall from Yale; Richard Stockton, Benjamin Rush, and Joseph Hewes from Princeton; Thomas Jefferson, Carter Braxton, Benjamin Harrison, and George Wythe from the College of William and Mary; Francis Hopkinson, James Smith, and William Paca from the College of Philadelphia; Thomas Nelson, Thomas Lynch, and Arthur Middleton from Cambridge; Francis Lewis from Westminster; John Witherspoon from the University of Edinburgh; James Wilson from the University of St. Andrews, the University of Glasgow, and the University of Edinburgh; and Charles Carroll of Carrollton from the Jesuit Seminaries of Rheimes and the College de St. Omer; additionally, Thomas McKean and George Read studied under the Rev. Dr. Allison, who later started the College of Philadelphia, and Thomas Heyward received private training that was the equivalent of an education taught in the most

respected seminaries (Charles Goodrich, *Lives of the Signers* (New York: William Reed & Co., 1829), p. 441). To learn more about the religious purposes of schools in the Founding Era such as Harvard, Yale, Princeton, *et al.*, see David Barton, *Original Intent: The Courts, the Constitution, & Religion* (Aledo, TX: WallBuilder Press, 2002), pp. 81-85.

123. See, for example, John Witherspoon, *Sermons on Practical Subjects* (Glasgow: A. Duncan and Company, 1768); *The Works of the Reverend John Witherspoon* (Philadelphia: William W. Woodward, 1802) (four volumes); *The Works of John Witherspoon* (Edinburgh: J. Ogle, 1815) (ten volumes); not to mention his individually published sermons and works, including *Christian Magnanimity* (Princeton: James Tod, 1787), *The Dominion of Providence Over the Passions of Men* (Philadelphia: R. Aitken, 1776), *Ecclesiastical Characteristics* (Philadelphia: Bradfords, 1767), and many others.

124. *The Holy Bible, Containing the Old and New Testaments* (Trenton: Isaac Collins, 1791), preface, "To The Reader," by John Witherspoon; see also Varnum Lansing Collins, *President Witherspoon: A Biography* (Princeton: Princeton University Press, 1925), p. 260.

125. *The Holy Bible, Containing the Old and New Covenants, Commonly Called the Old and New Testament: Translated from the Greek,* Charles Thomson, translator (Philadelphia: Jane Aitken, 1808).

126. L. H. Butterfield, "The Reputation of Benjamin Rush," *Pennsylvania History*, January 1950, Vol. XVII, No. 1, p. 9, John Adams to Richard Rush, May 5, 1813; see also *Delaplaine's Repository of the Lives and Portraits of Distinguished American Characters* (Philadelphia, 1815-1816), Vol. I, p. 42.

127. Galbraith Hall Todd, *The Torch and The Flag* (Philadelphia: American Sunday-School Union, 1966), p. 7.

128. *An Address of the Bible Society Established at Philadelphia to the Public* (Philadelphia: Fry and Kammerer, 1809), p. 24; John Owen, *The History of the Origin and First Ten Years of the British and Foreign Bible Society* (New York: James Eastburn & Co., 1817), p. 207.

129. *The Holy Bible Containing the Old and New Testaments Translated Out of the Original Tongues and with the Former Translations Diligently Compared and Revised* (London: T. Rutt, 1812).

130. *The Psalms of David, with the Ten Commandments, Creed, Lord's Prayer . . . Translated from the Dutch,* Francis Hopkinson, editor (New York: James Parker, 1767); see also Franklin, *Papers*, Vol. 12, p. 402, from Francis Hopkinson, December 13, 1765; George Everett Hastings, *The Life and Works of Francis Hopkinson* (Chicago: The University of Chicago Press, 1926), pp. 76-78.

131. James Wilson, Thomas M'Kean, *Commentaries on the Constitution of the United States of America* (London: J. Debrett, J. Johnson, J. S. Jordan, 1792).

132. A. J. Dallas, *Reports of Cases Ruled and Adjudged in the Courts of Pennsylvania* (Philadelphia: P. Byrne, 1806), Vol. I, p. 39, *Respublica v. John Roberts* (Pa. Sup. Ct. 1778).

133. William B. Reed, *Life and Correspondence of Joseph Reed* (Philadelphia: Lindsay and Blakiston, 1847), Vol. II, pp. 35-37, n.

134. From the Last Will & Testament of Samuel Adams, attested December 29, 1790.

135. From an autograph letter in our possession written by Charles Carroll to Charles W. Wharton, Esq., September 27, 1825.

136. Witherspoon, *Works*, Vol. V, pp. 276, 278, "The Absolute Necessity of Salvation Through Christ," January 2, 1758.

137. From the Last Will & Testament of Robert Treat Paine, attested May 11, 1814.

138. From the Last Will & Testament of Richard Stockton, attested May 20, 1780.

139. Benjamin Rush, *The Autobiography of Benjamin Rush*, George W. Corner, editor (Princeton: Princeton University Press, 1948), p. 166.

140. From the Last Will & Testament of John Dickinson, attested March 25, 1808.

141. Gunning Bedford, *Funeral Oration Upon the Death of General George Washington* (Wilmington: James Wilson, 1800), p. 18.

142. Lewis Henry Boutell, *The Life of Roger Sherman* (Chicago: A. C. McClurg and Company, 1896), pp. 272-273.

143. Jay, *Life of John Jay*, Vol. I, pp. 519-520, from his Last Will & Testament.

144. For example, the Rev. Jacob Duché himself prayed a ten-minute extemporary prayer at this meeting; see John Adams, *Letters of John Adams, Addressed to His Wife*, Charles Francis Adams, editor (Boston: Charles C. Little and James Brown, 1841), Vol. I, pp. 23-24, to Abigail Adams, September 16, 1774; see also Silas Deane, *The Deane Papers: Collections of the New York Historical Society for the Year 1886* (New York: Printed for the Society, 1887), Vol. I, p. 20, September 7, 1774; J. T. Headley *The Chaplains and Clergy of the Revolution* (Springfield, MA: G. & F. Bill, 1861), pp. 81-86.

145. John Adams, *Letters*, Vol. I, pp. 23-24, to Abigail Adams, September 16, 1774.

146. Deane, *Papers:*, Vol. I, p. 20, September 7, 1774; see also *Letters of Delegates*, Paul Smith, editor (Washington, DC: Library of Congress, 1976), Vol. I, p. 34, Silas Deane to Elizabeth Deane, September 7, 1774.

147. George Washington, *Address . . . Preparatory to his Declination*, pp. 22-23.

148. *Jane Doe v. Santa Fe Independent School District*, Civil Action No. G-95-176 (U.S.D.C., S.D. Tx. 1995) (court transcription of verbal ruling by federal judge Samuel Kent, pp. 3-4).

149. Madison, *Papers*, Vol. III, p. 1324, John Francis Mercer, August 14, 1787.

150. Madison, *Papers*, Vol. III, p. 1324, John Francis Mercer, August 14, 1787.

151. The 2000 census establishes 209 million voting age adults in America; the February 25 to March 10, 2002 Pew Research Center Survey ("2002 Religion and Public Life Survey") indicates that 29 percent of Americans consider themselves "born again, Evangelicals." Therefore, 29 percent of 209 million results in 60 million voting age Americans who would call themselves "born again, Evangelicals." The same Pew Research Survey establishes that over 10 million Evangelicals confess that they are not registered to vote, and an additional 2 million have inadvertently allowed their voter registration to lapse. This indicates that 12 million of the 60 million are not registered to vote, resulting in 20 percent of Evangelicals. The Republican National Committee conducted separate research, comparing lists of church members at Evangelical churches with voter registration files and found that a full 40 percent of Evangelicals were not registered to vote, resulting in a total of 24 million. While this number is almost twice as high as that reached by Pew, the difference in the two numbers can be attributed to suggested reasons such as many Evangelicals are ashamed to say they are not registered when questioned by surveyors.

152. From an autograph letter in our possession written by James A. Garfield, to Wallace Ford, February 16, 1858.

153. John M. Taylor, *Garfield of Ohio: The Available Man* (New York: W. W. Norton and Company, Inc., 1970), p. 180, quoted from "A Century of Congress," by James A. Garfield, *Atlantic*, July 1877.

154. Nancy Gibbs, "America's Holy War," *Time*, December 9, 1991, p. 64, *Time*/CNN Poll on Religion.

155. Gallup Organization, "Most Americans Support Prayer in Public Schools" (at http://www.gallup.com/poll/releases/pr990709.asp).

156. Gallup Organization, "Most Americans Support Prayer in Public Schools" (at http://www.gallup.com/poll/releases/pr990709.asp).

157. Gallup Organization, "Poll Topics & Trends: Abortion" (at http://www.gallup.com/poll/topics/abortion2.asp).

158. Charles G. Finney, *Lectures on Revivals of Religion* (New York: Fleming H. Revell Company, 1868, first published in 1835), Lecture XV, pp. 281-282.

159. Matthias Burnet, *An Election Sermon, Preached at Hartford, on the Day of the Anniversary Election, May 12, 1803* (Hartford: Hudson and Goodwin, 1803), pp. 26-27.

# Also Available from WallBuilders

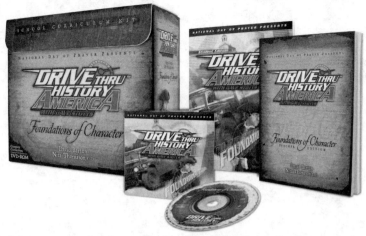

A history curriculum that unabashedly delivers the truth!
## Drive Through History America
written by David Barton & presented by award-winning actor Dave Stotts

# Visit our website for other great resources!

800-873-2845 • www.wallbuilders.com